Contents

Introduction

*P*EOPLE LOVE TO MAKE LISTS OF THE BIGGEST AND THE BEST. ALMOST 2,500 YEARS AGO, A GREEK HISTORIAN MADE A LIST OF THE GREATEST THINGS EVER BUILT. THE LIST INCLUDED BUILDINGS, STATUES AND OTHER OBJECTS THAT WERE LARGE, WONDROUS AND IMPRESSIVE. OTHER ANCIENT SCHOLARS ADDED THEIR OWN IDEAS TO THE LIST. SCHOLARS EVENTUALLY AGREED ON A FINAL LIST. IT WAS CALLED THE SEVEN WONDERS OF THE ANCIENT WORLD. THE ANCIENT WONDERS WERE:

THE GREAT PYRAMID AT GIZA: *a tomb for an ancient Egyptian king. The pyramid still stands in Giza, Egypt.*

THE COLOSSUS OF RHODES: *a giant bronze statue of Helios, the Greek sun god. The statue stood in Rhodes, an island in the Aegean Sea.*

THE LIGHTHOUSE OF ALEXANDRIA: *an enormous beacon to sailors at sea. It stood in the harbour in Alexandria, Egypt.*

THE HANGING GARDENS OF BABYLON: *magnificent gardens in the ancient city of Babylon (near modern-day Baghdad, Iraq).*

THE MAUSOLEUM AT HALICARNASSUS: *a marble tomb for a ruler in the Persian Empire. It was located in the ancient city of Halicarnassus (in modern Turkey).*

THE STATUE OF ZEUS AT OLYMPIA: *a statue honouring the king of the Greek gods. It stood in Olympia, Greece.*

THE TEMPLE OF ARTEMIS AT EPHESUS: *a temple built for a Greek goddess. It stood on the coast of the Aegean Sea, in modern-day Turkey.*

Most of these ancient wonders are no longer standing. They were destroyed by wars, earthquakes, weather and the passage of time.

Over the years, people made other lists of wonders. They listed wonders of the modern world and wonders of the natural world. They even listed wonders for each part of the Earth. This book is about ancient wonders from the Middle East.

A WONDERFUL PLACE

The Middle East includes lands around the eastern and south-eastern shores of the Mediterranean Sea. More than a dozen modern countries occupy this region. These countries include Egypt, Iran, Iraq, Saudi Arabia, Lebanon, Kuwait, Syria, Israel and Jordan.

People in ancient times never used the term *Middle East*. Instead, they called their region Mesopotamia. The name means 'between rivers'. Mesopotamia was between the Tigris and Euphrates rivers.

Mesopotamia is often called the cradle, or birthplace, of civilization. Mesopotamia had all the requirements for civilized life. The Tigris and Euphrates provided plenty of drinking water for many people. The rivers also provided water for growing wheat, barley and other farm crops. When the rivers overflowed their banks, they left layers of rich, black soil. This soil was good for growing crops.

In around 4000 BC, the ancient Sumerian people took advantage of the water and the rich soil. The Sumerians started one of the world's first civilizations. Other ancient civilizations also developed in the Middle East. These civilizations included Assyria, Babylonia and Persia.

A TRIP BACK IN TIME

Get ready to visit some of the wonders of the ancient Middle East. *Ancient* is another word for 'old'. This book will explore old cities, temples, monuments and other creations. Some of these wonders are thousands of years old. Others date back to the Middle Ages, the period between about AD 500 and 1500.

The first stop will be at giant towers that reached towards the heavens. A second stop will be one of the world's first libraries. Another place to visit on the journey will be a fantastic church. Some people believed that the church's enormous dome floated above the building. The wonders of the ancient Middle East are waiting.

This stairway leads to the top of the ziggurat (giant tower) at Ur (in what is modern-day Iraq).

SUMER WAS THE FIRST CIVILIZATION IN MESOPOTAMIA. SUMER WAS IN AN AREA THAT LATER BECAME IRAQ. THIS CIVILIZATION BEGAN ABOUT 4000 BC THE PEOPLE WHO LIVED THERE WERE CALLED SUMERIANS.

Sumer was not one big empire with one ruler. Instead, Sumer consisted of many small, independent kingdoms called city-states. Each city-state had its own ruler, government and army. Ur was one of the most powerful Sumerian city-states.

A king named Shulgi ruled Ur from about 2095 to 2047 BC. He lived in a beautiful palace. It sat on a wide street, surrounded by spacious courtyards. The city itself was surrounded by high walls, which protected Ur from its enemies.

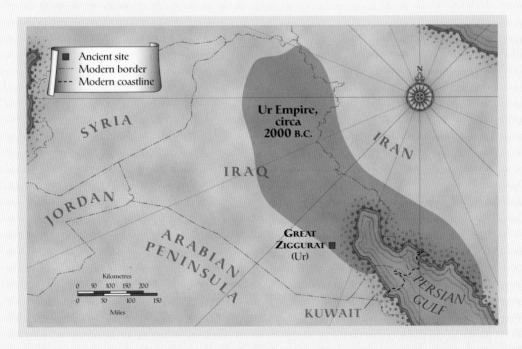

These bronze statuettes of King Shulgi are from Iraq and date to the late 2000s BC.

King Shulgi may have been the ancient world's biggest boaster. He made up stories about himself and spread them throughout the kingdom. One story claimed that Shulgi had once run 160 kilometres (100 miles) in two hours. If the story were true, he would have run nearly as fast as a modern car on a main road. Other stories said that the king was handsome, strong enough to kill lions with his bare hands and able to play every musical instrument.

BRIDGES TO HEAVEN

One of King Shulgi's accomplishments really was something to boast about. He finished building the Great Ziggurat of Ur. Ziggurats were giant towers found in Mesopotamian cities. The Great Ziggurat of Ur is the best-preserved monument from the ancient Sumerian civilization.

Ziggurats were taller than any other buildings in the city. They were wide at ground level and got narrower towards the top. They had wide terraces, or platforms, running along each side. The terraces looked like modern balconies or patios.

'Now, I swear by the sun god Utu on this very day . . . that I, the first-born son, am a fashioner of words, a composer of songs and they will recite my songs as heavenly writings and that they will bow down before my words.'

— King Shulgi, mid-2000s BC

One side of the ziggurat had a stairway. The stairway led to a temple at the top of the building. Sumerians thought of ziggurats as bridges between Earth and heaven. They climbed the stairway to be closer to their gods.

NANNA'S TEMPLE

The Great Ziggurat was the biggest building in Ur. It stood about 20 metres high. That's about as tall as a six-storey building. At its base, the ziggurat was about the size of two football pitches.

It was built on three levels, almost like a three-tiered wedding cake. The lowest level of the ziggurat was the widest. The second level was narrower than the first. That design created a terrace where the two levels met. The third level was smaller than the second, which created another terrace.

A temple sat on the very top of the ziggurat. It was a temple to the Sumerian god Nanna. Nanna was the ancient Sumerian moon god. He was also Ur's patron god. As patron, he protected the city from harm. King Shulgi and other rulers of Ur probably held big parades and ceremonies at the ziggurat to honour Nanna.

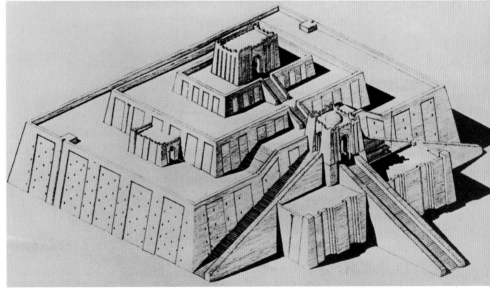

Left: *In this limestone carving, the Sumerian god Nanna holds objects that represent justice.* Right: *This drawing shows what the ziggurat would have looked like in the time of King Shulgi. The temple to Nanna is on the top.*

'On the summit [of the Great Ziggurat] there is a spacious shrine, inside which there is an exceptionally large bed, richly decorated with a golden table beside it. . . . They also say that the god [Nanna] comes to the room in person and sleeps on the bed. I do not believe it myself.'

— *Herodotus, a Greek historian, 400s BC*

Sumerian workers built the Great Ziggurat from bricks. The bricks were formed of mud and straw and then dried in the sun. A layer of harder bricks covered the outside. The workers used tar to hold the bricks in place. Shulgi's father started building the ziggurat during his reign. King Shulgi had the ziggurat finished.

HIGH ACHIEVER

In addition to completing the Great Ziggurat, Shulgi had other accomplishments. During his reign, he conquered nearby people. He expanded Ur's territory to include almost all of Sumer. Some historians say that Ur became the largest city in the world during Shulgi's rule. They think it had a population of almost sixty-five thousand people.

Shulgi built roads throughout his kingdom. He also built inns, or hotels. Travellers could eat, rest and sleep overnight at the inns during long trips.

When King Shulgi died, his sons became the rulers of Ur. Enemies constantly attacked the city. Shulgi's sons were not powerful warriors as their father had been. They could not protect the city. People called the Elamites conquered Ur around 2000 BC. The Sumerian civilization ended.

EVER *Wonder?*

How do we know exactly when King Shulgi ruled Ur? Ancient writings mention an eclipse of the sun that occurred during Shulgi's reign. (During an eclipse of the sun, the sun appears to go dark, because the moon has passed in front of it.) Scientists can date eclipses for thousands of years into the past. Scientists compared the dates of past eclipses to dates recorded in ancient texts. They concluded that Shulgi reigned for forty-eight years, from about 2095 to 2047 BC.

After Ur

The Great Ziggurat was not abandoned, however. Later groups, such as the Babylonians and the Assyrians, maintained the great building, and repaired the damage from wind and rain. The Babylonians enlarged the Great Ziggurat, adding four more levels.

Around 500 BC, people abandoned Ur. They might have left because of a drought or water shortage. People in other parts of Mesopotamia forgot about Ur. Over the centuries, the Great Ziggurat and other buildings in Ur were buried under windblown sand and dirt. Wind, rain and earthquakes damaged the buildings.

In the 1800s and 1900s, British and American archaeologists began to excavate,

In the 1800s and 1900s, archaeologists such as Sir Charles Leonard Woolley (inset) excavated the ziggurat. The photograph below was taken during Woolley's work between 1922 and 1934.

or dig around, the ruins at Ur. (Archaeologists study the remains of past cultures.) These archaeologists had to dig through more than 10 m of mud to uncover some of the ruins. They discovered the Great Ziggurat. They also discovered royal tombs, a temple and other ancient buildings.

By then Nanna's temple and other upper parts of the ziggurat had fallen apart. Archaeologists used ancient descriptions and drawings of the ziggurat to work out what it had looked like in ancient times. Archaeologists and the Iraqi government used this information to rebuild parts of the structure.

Archaeologists discovered other treasures in the ruins of Ur. They found jewellery made from gold and precious stones. They found golden statues and gold and silver cups. The archaeologists sent most of these treasures to museums in Great Britain and the United States of America. Historians studied the objects to learn more about life in ancient Sumer.

BIBLICAL *History*

The Bible is a collection of ancient writings. Some of the writings are sacred to both Jews and Christians. Others are sacred only to Christians. The Bible might offer some clues about ancient Ur. For instance, the Bible says that a man named Jacob fell asleep in the desert one night. He dreamed of a stairway that led from Earth to heaven *(in a nineteenth-century engraving below)*. Some modern scholars think that Jacob dreamed about a Sumerian ziggurat.

Another Bible story tells of a man named Abraham. He was born in a city called Ur Kasdim. Abraham led his family from Ur Kasdim to the land of Canaan (modern-day Israel). Abraham, his son and his grandson were the founders of the Jewish religion. Some scholars think that Ur Kasdim was another name for the city-state of Ur.

Archaeologists found many treasures from the city-state of Ur during digs near the Great Ziggurat. These treasures include a necklace made of carnelian (a red stone), lapis lazuli (a blue stone) and gold (above left); the sculpture known as Ram Caught in a Thicket (above right); a game board and game pieces (below left); and a gold cup (below right).

'I fell in love with Ur, with its beauty in the evening, the ziggurat standing up, faintly shadowed and that wide sea of sand with its lovely pale [colours] of apricot, rose, blue and mauve changing every minute.'
— novelist Agatha Christie, who used Mesopotamia as a setting for one of her novels

The Great Ziggurat is one of the few modern reminders of the great civilization of Sumer.

A MODERN WONDER

More than four thousand years after King Shulgi lived, ruins of the Great Ziggurat are still standing. The Great Ziggurat is one of the few big reminders of Ur in present-day Iraq.

In the early 2000s, the United States, Britain and other countries invaded Iraq. The US military set up a base near the ruins of Ur. The military also closed the ruins to the public. Until war ends in Iraq, tourists will not be able to visit the ruins. People who want to learn about Ur and the Great Ziggurat must do so through books, websites and museum exhibits. The British Museum in London and the University of Pennsylvania Museum of Archaeology and Anthropology in Philadelphia, USA, display many of the treasures of ancient Ur.

2 LIBRARY IN *Nineveh*

This gate once guarded the ancient city of Nineveh (in what is modern-day Iraq).

*A*LMOST THREE THOUSAND YEARS AGO, KING ASHURBANIPAL RULED THE ANCIENT EMPIRE OF ASSYRIA. NINEVEH WAS THE EMPIRE'S CAPITAL CITY. NINEVEH WAS IN MODERN-DAY IRAQ.

In ancient times, the city was filled with beautiful gardens. Some of the gardens were like small zoos. They were home to animals captured in distant lands. Workers dug canals and built pipes to bring water into Nineveh from the countryside.

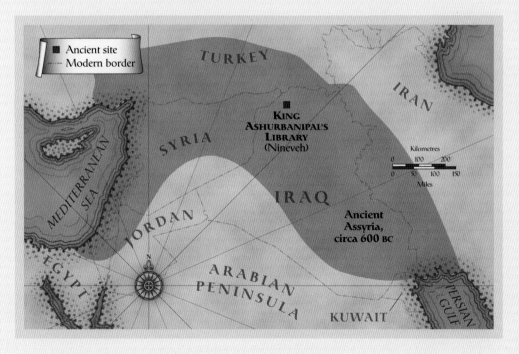

To protect the city from enemies, workers built a wall around Nineveh. The wall was more than 12 km (7.5 miles) long. Fifteen gates led into the city. Each gate had a strong door. Huge stone monsters guarded some of the gates. The monsters had the head of a man, the body of a bull and the wings of an eagle.

King Ashurbanipal was a fierce warrior. His soldiers often used cruelty and violence to frighten their enemies. Under Ashurbanipal's rule, in the 600s BC, Assyria reached the height of its power. It controlled much of the Middle East, including parts of Egypt, Syria, Babylonia and Palestine.

This modern drawing of the king's palace in Nineveh gives an idea of the magnificence of the Assyrian kingdom during the 700s and 600s BC.

This alabaster relief (carving) shows King Ashurbanipal killing a lion. Archaeologists found the relief in the king's North Palace in Nineveh.

Ashurbanipal lived in a magnificent palace. The palace doorways and walls were covered with carvings. They showed people, animals, kings and scenes from everyday life in Assyria. Some carvings showed Ashurbanipal hunting lions.

BOOKWORM KING

In addition to his military skills, King Ashurbanipal had an amazing talent. He could read and write. In those days, that skill was very unusual, even for a king. In ancient times, only a few people could read and write. These people were called scribes.

Scribes in the ancient Middle East did not write with paper and ink. They used a writing system called cuneiform. Using sharp sticks, they pressed letters into wet clay tablets. When the clay dried, the writing became permanent. The clay tablets were like books.

King Ashurbanipal was a bookworm. He loved reading and learning. He sent his scribes from the royal court in Nineveh to buy clay books from other parts of the Middle East. He set aside part of his palace as a place to keep the books. This place was one of the world's first libraries.

'Hidden treasures of all the knowledge of the scribes'
— *King Ashurbanipal's description of the clay tablets in his library, mid-600s BC*

Books and More Books

Among the tablets in Ashurbanipal's library were dictionaries, scientific works, reference books and lists of ancient kings. Some tablets contained descriptions of government, religion and everyday life. Other tablets contained stories dating back to the start of civilization in the Middle East. One story told about a giant flood that occurred in approximately 2300 BC. The story came from the ancient civilization of Sumer.

Another story was *The Epic of Gilgamesh*. This long poem tells of the adventures of Gilgamesh. He was a superhuman king. According to the story, Gilgamesh was part god and part human. In addition to Gilgamesh's

This cuneiform tablet tells part of The Epic of Gilgamesh.

King Ashurbanipal's library had some top-secret tablets. They were kept in top-secret reading rooms. These tablets contained information that spies had gathered about King Ashurbanipal's enemies and about other kingdoms. These reading rooms were off limits. Only scribes with special permission from the king could enter and read the secret tablets.

This clay tablet from Ashurbanipal's library contains a copy of the Code of Hammurabi – written laws proclaimed by King Hammurabi, who ruled the Babylonian Empire from 1792 BC to 1750 BC

adventures, the story also describes his feelings. It tells that he felt lonely, how he treated his friends and how he learned to behave in a civilized world. Like the flood story, *The Epic of Gilgamesh* came from Sumer.

King Ashurbanipal's library was organized like a modern library. Books were stored in different rooms according to subject. Some rooms were devoted to science, for instance. Others contained books on religion, government, history, poetry or geography. The library even had a card catalogue to help users locate books.

Users were not allowed to remove books from King Ashurbanipal's library. Some books were marked with warnings. The warnings said that anyone who stole the book would have bad luck.

'May [the goddess] Ishtar bless the reader who will not alter this tablet nor place it elsewhere in the library and may She denounce in anger he who dares withdraw it from the building.'
— a warning in a dictionary from King Ashurbanipal's library

The End of an Empire

King Ashurbanipal died in 627 BC. In 612 BC, the Babylonians destroyed Nineveh, including King Ashurbanipal's palace. The destruction of Nineveh put an end to the Assyrian Empire.

What happened to the clay tablets inside Ashurbanipal's library? They remained buried under the rubble of Ashurbanipal's palace. Over the centuries, wind-blown sand covered up the ruins. People still lived near Nineveh, but the city and the library were forgotten.

In the late 1840s, British archaeologist Austen Henry Layard began excavating ruins in the Middle East. Lavard unearthed Ashurbanipal's palace and library. Layard and other archaeologists found about twenty thousand clay tablets. They found a group of tablets containing *The Epic of Gilgamesh*. Some of the tablets in the ruins were badly broken. The archaeologists also found other artefacts, or objects, from ancient Nineveh.

Scholars studied the clay tablets. They translated the cuneiform writing into English and other modern languages. They realized that King Ashurbanipal's library was a priceless discovery. Without the tablets, modern people would know much less about ancient Assyria. Archaeologists sent many of the tablets from the palace to museums in Europe.

A Modern Wonder

Modern people who want to see clay tablets from King Ashurbanipal's library can view them in books, websites and museums. The British Museum in London and the Louvre Museum in Paris, France, display some of the tablets. The museums also display other artefacts from Nineveh. Modern-day scholars still translate and study the cuneiform writing to learn more about ancient Assyria.

Jigsaw Puzzle Tablets

Over many centuries, many of the clay tablets from the library at Nineveh broke into pieces. Some of them arrived at the British Museum like heaps of shattered dinner plates. Scientists at the museum worked for years to put the tablets back together. The work was almost like putting together jigsaw puzzles. Once the puzzles were together, they told important stories about life in the ancient Middle East.

ANOTHER *Library*

The most famous library in the ancient Middle East was in Alexandria, Egypt. That library contained texts written on papyrus, an early form of paper. The papyrus texts were rolled up into scrolls. The library at Alexandria was started in the 300s BC. At its height, it housed more than four hundred thousand scrolls.

Archaeologists think that large numbers of clay tablets remain in the ruins at Nineveh. However, few people can visit these ruins. Since 2003, war has been raging in Iraq. Bombs and bullets have damaged some of the buildings at Nineveh. Until the war in Iraq ends, the treasures remaining in the ruins will not be safe.

In modern times, visitors to Nineveh can still see the wall that surrounded the city. It was excavated and restored, along with the gates, at different times in the 1800s and 1900s.

3 Persepolis

The ruins of Persepolis (in Iran) sit on a stone terrace.

$\mathcal{I}$T WAS THE FIRST DAY OF SPRING.

ALMOST TEN THOUSAND PEOPLE CROWDED INTO THE AUDIENCE

HALL OF THE ROYAL PALACE. WHILE WAITING FOR THE SHOW TO

BEGIN, THE AUDIENCE MUST HAVE WHISPERED IN EXCITEMENT. FOR

A BETTER VIEW, SOME PEOPLE PROBABLY PEERED AROUND ONE

OF THE SEVENTY-TWO HUGE STONE COLUMNS THAT SUPPORTED

THE ROOF OF THIS GRAND ROOM. EACH COLUMN WAS HIGHER

THAN A TELEGRAPH POLE. EACH WAS CARVED WITH SCULPTURES

OF LIONS, EAGLES AND TWO-HEADED BULLS.

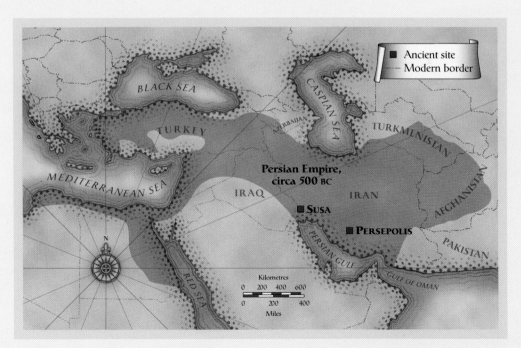

Finally, the show began. One by one, more than twenty rulers entered. They came from the empire's provinces, or local districts. Each ruler wore the brightly coloured clothing of his native land. They all carried expensive gifts for the man who ruled this great empire. Some of the local rulers brought gold and silver. Others carried jewels, weapons, beautiful woven cloth and pet animals.

TWO CAPITALS FOR A GREAT EMPIRE

This ceremony took place in the ancient city of Persepolis. Persepolis was one of

The ruins of Persepolis give an idea of the grandeur of the city before its destruction.

two capital cities of the ancient Persian Empire. The name *Persepolis* means 'city of the Persians'. Persepolis is in modern-day Iran.

From about 550 to 330 BC, Persia was the ancient world's largest and most powerful empire. It ruled a vast area of the Middle East. It stretched for thousands of kilometres, from the Mediterranean Sea eastwards to Afghanistan.

In ancient Persia, the first day of spring was New Year's Day. The ceremony in Persepolis was part of a grand New Year's festival. The celebration lasted for days. People held parades and parties. As part of the celebration, each ruler came to the capital city to show loyalty to the emperor of Persia.

Persia's other capital city was Susa. Susa was the government centre of the Persian Empire. There, people made laws and carried out government business. Persepolis was the empire's ceremonial centre. It was the place for crowning emperors and holding celebrations such as the spring festival.

This relief of Cyrus the Great stands in Pasargadae, Iran, the capital of the Persian Empire during Cyrus's reign (c 550-30 BC).

Darius the Great ruled Persia from 521 to 486 BC. He made Susa and Persepolis into capital cities soon after he came to power. The new capital cities replaced Pasargadae, the old capital. Pasargadae was the burial place of Cyrus the Great. Cyrus was the founder of the Persian Empire.

A DIFFERENT KIND OF WARRIOR

Before he was an emperor, Cyrus was the chief of a small tribe. He lived in southern Persia. He began building his empire in 559 BC. He conquered the Medians, the Babylonians and other ancient civilizations. Soon, Persia was the largest empire in the ancient world.

Cyrus's army was his secret weapon. Other armies fought mainly face-to-face and on the ground. Soldiers on foot slashed and hacked at the enemy with swords and axes.

However, Cyrus's armies attacked from a distance. His archers stood in safety, far away from the enemy. They shot hundreds of arrows at the enemy. When the terrified enemy soldiers tried to retreat, Cyrus attacked with swarms of cavalry, or soldiers on horseback.

In ancient times, victorious leaders often destroyed the cities they conquered. They either killed the people who lived there or turned them into slaves. Cyrus was different. He treated conquered people kindly and fairly. For instance, after conquering Babylon in 539 BC, Cyrus freed the Jewish people, whom the Babylonians had forced to live there. Cyrus allowed the Jews to return to their home city of Jerusalem.

EXPANDING THE EMPIRE

When Cyrus died in 530 BC, his son Cambyses II took over the Persian Empire. Cambyses expanded the empire by conquering Egypt. Persia's next ruler was Darius the Great, who continued to expand the empire. Darius divided the empire into provinces. Each province had a ruler called a satrap. The provinces had to pay taxes to the emperor.

Persepolis was an important part of Darius's empire. Darius wanted Persepolis to be a symbol of Persian unity. He wanted to show off his

CYRUS'S *Cylinder*

In 1879 archaeologists found a clay cylinder in the ruins of ancient Babylon. The cylinder *(below)* is marked with cuneiform text. It was written shortly after Cyrus conquered Babylon in 539 BC. The text tells of the misdeeds of the previous king of Babylon and the good deeds of Cyrus, such as allowing the Jews to return to Jerusalem. The charter states, in part, 'I announce that I will respect the traditions, customs and religions of the nations of my empire and never let any of my governors and [staff] look down on or insult them [while] I am alive. . . . I will never let anyone oppress any others, and if it occurs, I will . . . penalize [punish] the oppressor.' Some modern scholars have called these words the world's first declaration of human rights. Cyrus's cylinder is on display at the British Museum in London.

wealth, power and greatness there. He wanted the satraps to come to Persepolis honour him.

Darius began building Persepolis around 518 BC, but the city was not completed until almost one hundred years later. Darius's son Xerxes became emperor in 486 BC Xerxes oversaw much of the construction of Persepolis.

The centre of Persepolis held an enormous stone terrace. The terrace was 450 m long and 300 m wide. It was almost as long as five football pitches and as wide as three football pitches. Rising from the terrace were magnificent palaces, meeting halls and other buildings for Persia's rulers.

The palace of Darius is one of the best-preserved buildings at Persepolis.

Stories say that the buildings overflowed with gold, silver, jewels and other riches.

People entered the terrace by climbing a wide stairway. The stairway passed through a gigantic stone gatehouse, which was guarded by stone statues of monsters. After passing through the gatehouse, people reached the royal palace. The palace was the largest and most magnificent building in Persepolis.

This photo (below) of the stone terrace was taken during excavations in the early 1900s. The columns are the remains of the Audience Hall, and the doorways on the far right mark Darius's palace. The gatehouse can be seen at left and in the inset.

This is a model of what the terrace of Persepolis may have looked like.

Inside it was the Audience Hall, where rulers of Persian provinces came with gifts to honour the emperor.

ALEXANDER'S REVENGE

Persia had many enemies. One enemy was the Greeks. The two empires fought with each other for many years. In one war, in 480 BC, a Persian army burned the Greek city of Athens. The Persians destroyed beautiful temples and monuments on the Acropolis, a famous hill at the centre of Athens.

The Greeks wanted revenge against Persia. In 334 BC, a Greek general named Alexander invaded Persia. Alexander conquered Persepolis in 330 BC. Before leaving Persepolis, Alexander took revenge. He gathered all the city's gold and silver to take home with him. There was so much treasure that Alexander needed twenty thousand mules and five thousand camels to carry it away. Alexander burned the royal palace and other buildings on the terrace. The destruction of Persepolis ended the Persian Empire.

Some people continued to live in Persepolis, even after the destruction, but gradually they moved away. Persepolis became a ghost town. Some of the buildings crumbled. Blowing sand covered up the ruins.

Persepolis

'*Just as Persepolis had surpassed other cities in prosperity [richness], so too it surpassed them in misfortune!*'

— *ancient Greek historian Diodorus Siculus, writing about the destruction of Persepolis, first century BC*

A MODERN WONDER

For two thousand years, no one paid much attention to Persepolis. Finally, in the 1930s, archaeologists began to excavate the ruins. The Iranian government restored some of the ancient buildings.

The people of modern Iran are proud of their ancient Persian heritage. In 1971 Iranian rulers hosted a grand celebration at Persepolis. The event celebrated the founding of the Persian Empire twenty-five hundred years earlier.

In 1979 UNESCO (the United Nations Educational, Scientific and Cultural Organization) declared Persepolis to be a World Heritage Site. World Heritage Sites are cities, buildings, monuments and other places that have special historical importance for mankind.

Thousands of tourists from Iran and elsewhere visit Persepolis each year. Visitors can walk among the ruins of this ancient wonder. However, they are not allowed to touch the ancient buildings or statues.

ANCIENT *Postmen*

Before postmen and the Royal Mail, all letters and post in Britain was handled by messengers. These men delivered mail on horseback, using post stations around the country to rest while travelling. In the 400s BC, riders on horseback carried messages throughout the Persian Empire. They switched horses at 111 stations scattered across the empire.

In 1971 Iranian rulers built a replica of the famous staircase from Persepolis and displayed it in a square in Tehran, the modern capital of Iran.

Many tourists visit the ruins of Persepolis (below). A modern city can be seen beneath the mountains in the distance.

4 King Solomon's TEMPLE

King Solomon dedicates the temple in Jerusalem in this print from the 1870s.

$\mathcal{T}$HE ANCIENT KINGDOM OF ISRAEL WAS A JEWISH KINGDOM IN THE MIDDLE EAST. ITS CAPITAL CITY WAS JERUSALEM. DAVID, AN ISRAELITE KING, WANTED TO BUILD A TEMPLE IN JERUSALEM TO HOUSE THE ARK OF THE COVENANT. ACCORDING TO THE BIBLE, THE ARK WAS A SACRED CHEST. IT WAS SAID TO CONTAIN STONE TABLETS ON WHICH GOD HAD WRITTEN THE TEN COMMANDMENTS.

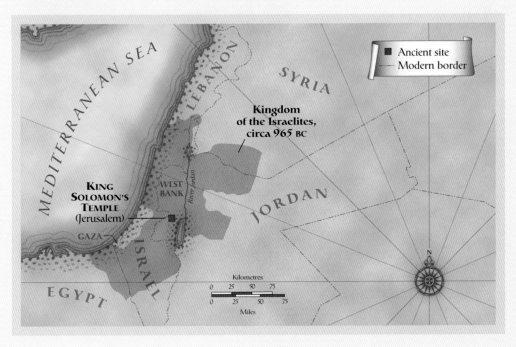

However, a message from God said that David could not build the temple because he was a warrior who had killed people. So David decided that his son Solomon would build the temple. David left Solomon money for building the temple.

In those days, people used gold and silver as money. Stories in the Bible suggest that it would have taken about one million men to carry all the silver and one hundred thousand men to carry all the gold that Solomon used to build his temple.

TALENTED *Money*

People in the ancient Middle East did not just count money. They also weighed it in units called talents. A talent was about as much as a strong man could carry – about 35 kilograms. The Bible says that King David left Solomon one hundred thousand talents of gold and one million talents of silver to build the First Temple. At modern prices, one talent of gold is worth about £330,000. A talent of silver is worth about £3,500. In modern money, that comes out to more than £35 billion to build the temple.

King Solomon receives a visit from the queen of Sheba. According to the Bible and the Quran (the holy book of Islam), both Solomon and the queen were fantastically wealthy rulers.

King David (with harp) *leads priests carrying the Ark of the Covenant. This image is from the 1800s.*

In 965 BC, King Solomon built the temple on top of Mount Moriah in Jerusalem. For Jews this is a holy place. According to the Bible, God had tested the faith of Abraham, the father of the Jewish people, at this site.

Stories describe Solomon's Temple as a magnificent place of worship for the Jews of Jerusalem. People also gathered at the temple to socialize, discuss politics, and trade goods. One room in the building housed the Ark of the Covenant. The room was called the Holy of Holies.

According to the Bible, Solomon's Temple was one of the ancient world's grandest buildings. The temple stood in the centre of a paved plaza. It had three entrance gates. A porch in front of the temple was covered with pure gold.

In 586 BC, the Babylonians conquered Jerusalem. They destroyed Solomon's Temple. They forced the Jews to move to Babylon. In 539 BC, Cyrus the Great conquered the Babylonians. Cyrus allowed the Jews to move back home to Jerusalem. The Jews rebuilt Solomon's Temple. The rebuilt temple was called the Second Temple. Stories say that it was a plain and simple building at first.

A BIGGER, BETTER TEMPLE

In the first century BC, the Romans conquered Jerusalem and the surrounding lands. The Romans put a king named Herod in charge of the region. Herod

> *'He who has not seen the Temple of Herod has never seen a beautiful building. Of what did he build it? . . . Of yellow and white marble. Some say of blue, yellow and white marble . . . looking like the waves of the sea.'*
> — *The Babylonian Talmud, a book of Jewish law, c AD 500*

was a great builder. In 20 BC, he decided to remodel and enlarge the Second Temple. The project took more than forty years.

To strengthen the temple, King Herod built a stone wall around the bottom. He also cleared an area around the temple. It was almost as big as forty football pitches. Workers paved the area with stones. Then created a huge stone plaza around the temple.

In AD 66, the Jewish people revolted against Roman rule. Fighting continued for several years. In AD 70, Roman soldiers destroyed Jerusalem, including the Second Temple. The only part of the temple that remained was the western section of Herod's wall. It became known as the Western Wall. Some stories say that Roman soldiers allowed the Western Wall to remain standing as a reminder of their victory.

THE TEMPLE MOUNT

The site of King Solomon's Temple became known as the Temple Mount. Not only is this site sacred to Jews, it is also sacred to Christians. Christians believe that Jesus preached at the site in the early years of the first century AD The Christian religion is based on Jesus's teachings. In the early centuries AD, the Christian religion spread throughout the Mediterranean world.

In the AD 600s, another new religion – Islam – emerged in the Middle East. People who practise Islam are called Muslims. Muslims believe that in AD 621,

BUS-SIZED *Stone*

King Herod's workers used gigantic blocks of stone to build the wall around the bottom of the Second Temple. One block is larger than all the others. It is the size of a single-decker bus. It is 13 m long, 13.5 m high, and 4.5 m deep. It weighs about 550,000 kg. The stone is still visible in the Western Wall.

the prophet Muhammad ascended to heaven from a huge rock on the Temple Mount. So the Temple Mount also became sacred to Muslims. Later in the 600s, Muslims constructed the Dome of the Rock on the Temple Mount. This shrine was named after the rock on which Muhammad had stood.

The Dome of the Rock, also known as the Omar Mosque (place of worship), stands where Solomon's Temple once stood. The dome is a sacred site for Muslims.

The Western Wall

By the 700s, the Western Wall had become an important place of worship for Jews. Pilgrims travelled long distances to Jerusalem to pray at the wall and to recall the destruction of the Second Temple. To some people, the praying sounded like crying. That's how the wall earned another name, the Wailing Wall.

As the centuries passed, people built homes and other buildings near the Western Wall. Most of the wall became hidden beneath dirt and stones. By the twentieth century, only a small part of the wall was visible. It was in a narrow alley, barely 4 m wide. Only a few hundred worshippers could fit into the alley at one time.

In the twentieth century, Muslims and Jews fought for control of Jerusalem. The Jews created a new nation – Israel – in the Middle East in 1948. In 1967 Israel took control of Jerusalem and the Western Wall.

Israeli leaders wanted to give worshippers better access to the wall. They cleared away some of the buildings near it. They created the Western Wall Plaza.

Above: *Worshippers gather at the Western Wall in Jerusalem in 1910. At the time, space around the wall was limited.* **Below:** *Israeli soldiers rejoice at the Western Wall after capturing part of Jerusalem during the Six Day War in 1967.*

The new plaza had room for tens of thousands of worshippers. The Israelis also dug below the street. They exposed layers of the wall that had been buried for centuries. Where workers could not expose the wall completely, they dug tunnels. The tunnels allow people to view underground sections of the wall.

Below: *Pilgrims gather in the Western Wall Plaza.*
Right: *A Jewish man visits a newly opened tunnel by the Western Wall in the late 1990s.*

A Jewish man prays at the Western Wall. Many Jews leave prayers written on paper in the cracks of the wall.

A MODERN WONDER

The Western Wall and the Temple Mount are still holy places to people of the Christian, Muslim and Jewish faiths. Christians visit the Temple Mount to see places that were important in Jesus's life and in the creation of the Christian Church. Muslims come to visit the Dome of the Rock. They also come to visit an ancient mosque, or Islamic house of worship, near the wall.

At one section of the Western Wall, Jews can be seen at all hours of the day and night. Some pray silently. Others chant. Some worshippers place bits of paper with written prayers in cracks between the stone blocks. Some of those prayers ask for construction of a new temple, something very important in the Jewish faith. Jews also hold religious ceremonies at the wall.

In 1981 the United Nations declared the entire Old City (ancient portion) of Jerusalem to be a UNESCO World Heritage Site. However, Jerusalem and the areas surrounding the city are also the centre of conflict between Jews and Muslims. So although it is a sacred place, the Temple Mount is also a place of tension.

The mosque known as the Dome of the Rock can be seen just past the Western Wall in Jerusalem. In modern times, the site of Solomon's Temple is a holy site to three of the world's religions: Judaism, Islam and Christianity.

5 Petra

Tourists in Jordan peer into the door of the largest carved building in the ancient city of Petra. The building is a tomb commonly known as the Monastery.

$\mathcal{I}$N 1812, A SWISS EXPLORER NAMED JOHANN BURCKHARDT RODE ON HORSEBACK THROUGH THE SCORCHING HOT DESERT OF PRESENT-DAY JORDAN. A LOCAL GUIDE RODE WITH HIM. AFTER HOURS OF TRAVEL, THEY ENTERED A NARROW, DARK AND SPOOKY CANYON.

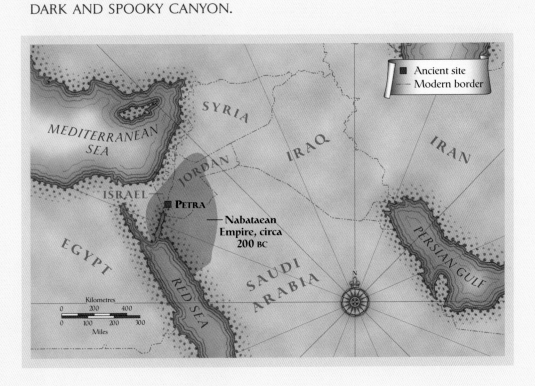

The canyon was a crack that snaked through a mountain. It twisted and turned to form a natural passageway. The canyon walls were as high as a twenty-storey building in some places. The two canyon walls were so close together that Burckhardt could barely see the sky. Noises echoed off the rocky canyon walls. Stones and sand tumbled down from above.

Finally, the canyon widened. Burckhardt and his guide emerged into a sunlit valley. Burckhardt could not believe his eyes. Straight ahead, he saw an enormous building in the valley. It looked just like an ancient Greek or Roman temple. It was higher than a twelve-storey building and almost 30 m wide. It was beautifully carved into the rock of the valley walls.

The building had towering columns, with larger-than-life statues of ancient gods and goddesses. The building also had statues of eagles, vines and monsters with snakes attached to their heads. The building and the statues glowed in the sunlight in shades of red, rose, pink and orange.

Continuing ahead, Burckhardt discovered an entire stone city hidden in the canyon. He found more buildings carved into the sandstone cliffs and more magnificent temples. He even found an enormous open-air theatre. It had benches for spectators and a stage carved entirely out of the rock. Later, Burckhardt described his discovery as 'one of the most elegant remains of antiquity [ancient times].'

Burckhardt entered the city of Petra through this canyon in 1812. The towering columns of the temple are visible at the end of the canyon.

This amphitheatre in Petra has seating for nearly six thousand people.

Burckhardt had just rediscovered Petra, one of the ancient world's most remarkable cities. People in Europe were excited when he told them about a mysterious city carved from stone.

ROCKY *Architecture*

Creating buildings by carving into cliffs and mountains is called rock-cut architecture. Besides the Nabataeans, other ancient people also built this way. Around AD 1200, the Anasazi people of the south-western United States made rock-cut buildings. People in ancient India and Turkey also made rock-cut buildings.

DESERT OASIS

Petra was the capital of the ancient Nabataean civilization. The Nabataean kingdom included parts of modern-day Jordan and Syria. The Nabataeans were wanderers who moved into the area in about 600 BC. In the 400s BC, they began to settle down and live in villages.

Petra was the perfect place for the headquarters of their empire. The city was easy to defend because the only entrances were through narrow canyons. Soldiers could hide on top of cliffs and throw rocks and spears down onto enemies.

Petra was also near an important caravan route. Caravans were groups of traders who carried silk, spices and other goods between Asia and the Middle East. They used camels to carry their heavy loads. The Nabataeans made caravans pay to pass through their land. The Nabataeans also sold food and water to the travellers.

Petra is dry for most of the year, but it sometimes gets heavy rains. The Nabataeans built a water supply system to save rainwater for drinking and washing. They built canals and pipes to carry the rainwater to stone reservoirs (ponds) and storage chambers. A nearby spring also supplied Petra with water. Within the city, the Nabataeans used clay pipes to carry water to people's homes. Even in the driest times, Petra had plenty of water from the reservoirs and spring. Petra was an oasis – a wet, green spot in the desert.

By the 200s BC, Petra was one of the most famous cities in the ancient world. People from as far away as China told stories about this magnificent city of stone, with its palaces, temples and monuments. The city covered 45 sq km (17 sq miles). It had more than five hundred monuments and other buildings.

NOTEWORTHY
Nabataeans

The Nabataean writing system was difficult and confusing. Letters could have different shapes depending on their place in a word. Writers didn't leave spaces between words. Some words started on one line and continued on the next without any hyphen. As difficult as it was, the Nabataean writing system is noteworthy. It became the basis of modern Arabic writing. Hundreds of millions of people living in the Middle East and elsewhere use the Arabic writing system.

The Nabataeans built channels like this one to bring water into the city of Petra.

'We do not know with what to compare this scene.
Perhaps there is nothing in the world that resembles it.'
— *British naval officers Charles Irby and James Mangles,*
describing the Khazneh (Treasury), 1818

THE PHARAOH'S TREASURY

What building had Johann Burckhardt seen when he first emerged from that dark, narrow canyon? It was the Khazneh, or Treasury – the most magnificent building in Petra. The Khazneh looked like an ancient Greek temple. The Nabataeans probably borrowed the idea for the design from the ancient Greeks. The two groups visited, and traded with, each other.

The Khazneh (Treasury) has some of the most detailed carvings in Petra.

The name Treasury came from a fantastic story about an ancient Egyptian pharaoh (king). The story said that the pharaoh used magic to build Petra as a storage place for his treasure. The treasure was supposed to be hidden in a secret chamber in the Khazneh. Modern archaeologists know that the legend of the pharaoh's treasure cannot be true. The Khazneh was probably built in about AD 25, long after the end of the ancient Egyptian Empire and the time of the pharaohs. In addition, the Khazneh was probably built as a temple or a royal tomb rather than a place to store treasure.

SHOOTING FOR *Treasure*

In earlier centuries, many people believed the legend of the pharaoh's treasure. Sometimes people shot guns at the front of the Khazneh. They hoped to hit a magic button that would open the secret chamber that they believed held the treasure.

ADVANCE AND DECLINE

Originally, the Nabataeans had their own name for their stone city. The Romans and Greeks called the city Petra, which means 'rock' in the ancient Greek language. In AD 106, the Roman Empire took control of Petra. The Roman emperor Hadrian visited the city in AD 131. He renamed the city in his own honour. He called it Petra Hadriane. Modern people use the name Petra.

The Romans improved and enlarged the city's water system. They made it large enough to supply water to thirty thousand people. Roman builders made other improvements. For instance, they built a paved road along the caravan route.

'It is astonishing that a people should . . . have carved the living rock into temples, [theatres], public and private buildings and tombs, and have thus constructed a city on the borders of the desert.'

— British archaeologist Austen Henry Layard, 1887

Left: *The interior of the Khazneh is a simple square room cut out of the rock.* Above: *This stone sculpture with Nabataean writing on the bottom was found at Petra.* Below: *These buildings are small tombs for the less wealthy residents of Petra.*

EVER *Wonder?*

How did Nabataean workers carve an entire city out of solid rock? The canyon walls around Petra are made of sandstone. That rock is softer and easier to cut than other kinds of stone. Petra's sculptors probably drew patterns on the sides of the cliffs. Then they carefully carved the patterns deeper and deeper into the rock. Workers probably carved buildings from the roof down. In that way, they avoided sharp chips of stone falling on their heads.

This walkway through the caves of Petra shows the rich red stone out of which the city was carved.

NEW *Wonders*

In 2007 a group in Switzerland held a contest. It asked people to vote online for the New Seven Wonders of the World. More than 100 million people voted. Petra was one of the winners. The other wonders were:

- **The Colosseum, an ancient amphitheatre in Rome, Italy**
- **Chichén Itzá, an ancient city in Mexico, created by the Mayan people**
- **Machu Picchu, an ancient city in Peru, created by the Incan people**
- **The Taj Mahal, a palace in India**
- **The Great Wall of China, a wall that snakes across part of northern China**
- **Christ the Redeemer, a huge statue of Jesus in Rio de Janeiro, Brazil**

Petra began to decline in the early centuries AD. New trade routes replaced the old caravan routes, so fewer traders came to Petra. Earthquakes damaged the city in AD 363 and 551.

By the 700s, the city was practically abandoned. The only visitors were local animal herders. They used the stone buildings as shelters while travelling in the area. Johann Burckhardt was the first European visitor to Petra in many centuries. Soon other Europeans arrived to marvel at the stone city. Archaeologists began to excavate the ruins of Petra in the early 1900s.

A MODERN WONDER

Petra became a tourist attraction in the twentieth century. In 1985 UNESCO declared Petra to be a World Heritage Site. In the twenty-first century, Petra is one of the most popular places to visit in Jordan. It is part of a national park, protected by Jordan's government. Rain and wind-blown sand have damaged some of the buildings over the centuries. But others, including the Khazneh, look much as they did in ancient times.

Thousands of tourists visit this ancient wonder every year. At the same time, archaeologists still excavate the ruins.

'A rose-red city, half as old as Time'
— from a poem about Petra by John William Burgon, 1845

Hagia Sophia

Emperor Justinian I built Hagia Sophia in Constantinople (modern-day Istanbul, Turkey) between AD 532 and 537.

$\mathcal{B}$Y THE THIRD AND FOURTH CENTURIES AD, THE POWERFUL ROMAN EMPIRE BEGAN TO DECLINE. EVENTUALLY, THE EMPIRE SPLIT INTO A WESTERN PART AND AN EASTERN PART. THE EASTERN PART BECAME THE BYZANTINE EMPIRE. ITS CAPITAL CITY WAS CONSTANTINOPLE, NAMED AFTER THE EMPEROR CONSTANTINE. IN MODERN TIMES, CONSTANTINOPLE IS THE CITY OF ISTANBUL, TURKEY.

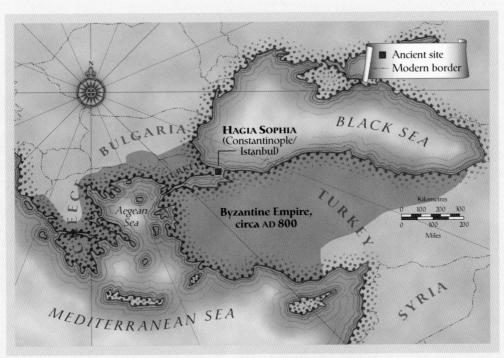

Ancient site
Modern border

BULGARIA

BLACK SEA

HAGIA SOPHIA
(Constantinople/
Istanbul)

GREECE

TURKEY

Aegean
Sea

**Byzantine Empire,
circa AD 800**

TURKEY

Kilometres
0 100 200 300
0   400   200
Miles

MEDITERRANEAN SEA

SYRIA

'O, Solomon, I have surpassed thee.'
— *Emperor Justinian, comparing Hagia Sophia to King Solomon's Temple in Jerusalem, AD 537*

In ancient times, many countries had an official religion, which every citizen had to practise. The official religion of the Byzantine Empire was Christianity. In 532 Byzantine emperor Justinian I ordered construction of a grand new cathedral in Constantinople. Justinian wanted the large church to show off the power of his government and the Christian faith. The cathedral would be used for crowning kings and for other important events.

The church was called Hagia Sophia, or the Church of Holy Wisdom. (*Hagia* means 'holy', and *sophia* means 'wisdom' in Greek.) The church was meant to honour the wisdom of the Christian God. When it was built, it was the biggest church in the world. It covered an area the size of two football pitches.

MAKING A DOME FLOAT

Justinian hired architects to design the church. The design required all of their talent because Justinian wanted Hagia Sophia to include a giant dome.

Building the dome of Hagia Sophia was a big challenge for ancient engineers.

EVER *Wonder?*

How long did it take to build Hagia Sophia? Considering how big it is and that workers in those days did not have modern machinery, the church was completed in an amazingly short time. It took just five years, ten months and four days to build. Justinian hired almost ten thousand labourers to build the church. They worked from sunrise to sunset, and they got paid extra for finishing their work on time.

A dome is a circular roof. It looks like a bowl turned upside down on top of a building.

In those days, building workers had no modern machinery. They had no cranes to lift heavy building materials high above the ground. Building a big dome was especially difficult. Workers had to stack bricks into a curved shape. Sometimes the bricks wouldn't stay in place. The bricks fell, and the whole dome tumbled down.

To support a massive dome, the Hagia Sophia architects invented a new support system. The architects built four massive pillars at the centre of the church. They built curved structures called arches on top of the pillars. The arches carried the weight of the dome downwards, so that it rested on the church's base.

In a stroke of creative genius, the designers pierced the base of the dome with forty curved windows. Light streaming through the windows created a special effect. The dome seemed to float above the lower part of the church. Golden tiles lined the interior of the dome. These tiles changed the colour of the incoming sunlight. The light looked as if it were glowing.

'Upon this circle rests the huge spherical [globe-shaped] dome which makes the structure exceptionally beautiful. Yet it seems not to rest upon solid masonry [bricks], but to cover the space with its golden dome suspended from Heaven.'

— *Procopius, a Byzantine historian, AD 500s*

Hagia Sophia was magnificent in other ways. It had gold and silver decorations inside. The walls were covered with mosaics – pictures made from millions of tiny pieces of coloured stone. Some of the mosaics showed Emperor Justinian and his wife, Empress Theodora. Others showed church leaders and holy men. Some mosaics showed famous people from the Bible.

Hagia Sophia was completed in AD 537. With its magical dome and colourful mosaics, it was the grandest church in the Christian world. People who saw the church told a fantastic story about the dome. They said

Left: *This mosaic of Jesus is in Hagia Sophia.* Below: *In another mosaic, Mary, Jesus' mother, holds her son. Emperor Justinian (left)* displays a model of Hagia Sophia and Emperor Constantine *(right)* holds a model of the city of Constantinople.

'It is impossible accurately to describe the gold, and silver and gems [in Hagia Sophia] . . . but by the description of one part, I leave the rest to be [worked out]. That part of the church which is especially sacred and where the priests alone are allowed to enter, which is called the Sanctuary, contains forty thousand pounds' [18,000 kg] weight of silver.'

— Procopius, AD 500s

that the dome was not attached to the church. They claimed that it floated on a ring of light. Some people called it the Floating Dome of Heaven.

Of course, the dome did not really float. It was big and heavy. It was almost 31 m across. It towered 56 m above the church floor. The dome was built from bricks, like a modern brick wall. It was incredibly heavy.

FROM CHURCH TO MOSQUE TO MUSEUM

In the 550s, two earthquakes struck Constantinople. The quakes damaged Hagia Sophia. In 558 the dome collapsed. Workers built a new dome and repaired the other damage. Christians continued to worship at Hagia Sophia for almost nine hundred more years.

Ottomans, who were Muslims, conquered Constantinople in 1453. They turned Hagia Sophia into a mosque. They painted over the mosaics that showed Christian images. Outside the church, they built four minarets, or towers. Five times a day, men would climb the minarets. From the top, they would call their fellow Muslims to prayer.

Hagia Sophia served Muslim worshippers for almost five hundred years. In 1935 the government of Turkey turned Hagia Sophia into a museum instead of a mosque. Workers uncovered the Christian mosaics and restored the church to its old appearance. However,

WORLD'S BIGGEST *Church*

Hagia Sophia was the biggest church in the world for almost one thousand years. In 1519 people in Seville, Spain, finished the Seville Cathedral, an even bigger church.

restorers took care to preserve the Muslim features of the building as well as the Christian ones. In that way, Hagia Sophia honours both the Christian and Muslim faiths.

A MODERN WONDER

The Hagia Sophia Museum is among modern Istanbul's most famous landmarks. Every day thousands of tourists from around the world come to admire this modern wonder. The Turkish government maintains and preserves the building. Hagia Sophia and other historic buildings in Istanbul are protected as UNESCO World Heritage Sites.

However, this fantastic building faces several threats. Air pollution eats away at the stones and bricks on the building's exterior. The thousands of daily visitors pose another threat. When people exhale, or breathe out, they release moisture into the air. All this moisture can damage the mosaics and decorations inside the church. For the people of Turkey, Hagia Sophia is a national treasure. The Turkish people are determined to solve these problems and preserve Hagia Sophia for future generations.

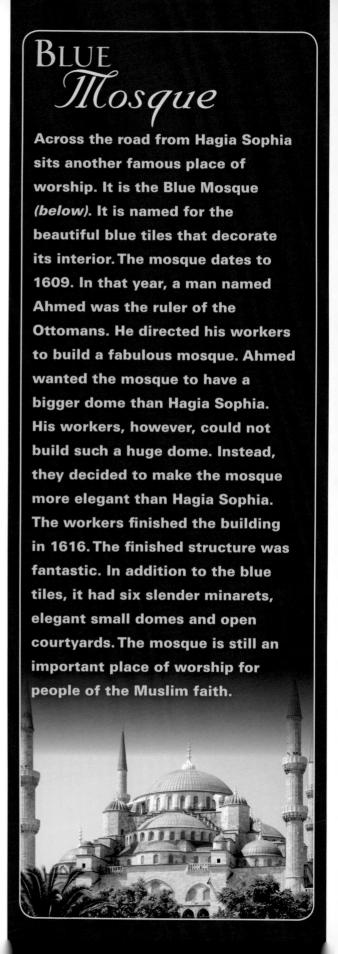

BLUE Mosque

Across the road from Hagia Sophia sits another famous place of worship. It is the Blue Mosque *(below)*. It is named for the beautiful blue tiles that decorate its interior. The mosque dates to 1609. In that year, a man named Ahmed was the ruler of the Ottomans. He directed his workers to build a fabulous mosque. Ahmed wanted the mosque to have a bigger dome than Hagia Sophia. His workers, however, could not build such a huge dome. Instead, they decided to make the mosque more elegant than Hagia Sophia. The workers finished the building in 1616. The finished structure was fantastic. In addition to the blue tiles, it had six slender minarets, elegant small domes and open courtyards. The mosque is still an important place of worship for people of the Muslim faith.

Top: *This photograph of the exterior of Hagia Sophia gives an impression of the immense size of the building.*
Bottom: *Hagia Sophia (building in background with minarets) and the Blue Mosque (building in foreground) are both in the centre of Istanbul.*

7 KRAK DES *Chevaliers*

Krak des Chevaliers is in the modern country of Syria. It is a well-protected castle meant to withstand sieges (military attacks).

SEVERAL TIMES DURING THE LATE MIDDLE AGES (AD 1100–1300), CHRISTIAN KNIGHTS MARCHED FROM EUROPE TO THE MIDDLE EAST. THESE KNIGHTS WERE CALLED CRUSADERS. THE MIDDLE EAST IS SACRED TO CHRISTIANITY BECAUSE IT IS THE BIRTHPLACE OF JESUS AND CHRISTIANITY. CHRISTIANS CALL IT THE HOLY LAND. THE CRUSADERS OF THE LATE MIDDLE AGES WANTED TO RECAPTURE THIS HOLY TERRITORY FROM MUSLIMS, WHO RULED THE HOLY LAND AT THAT TIME.

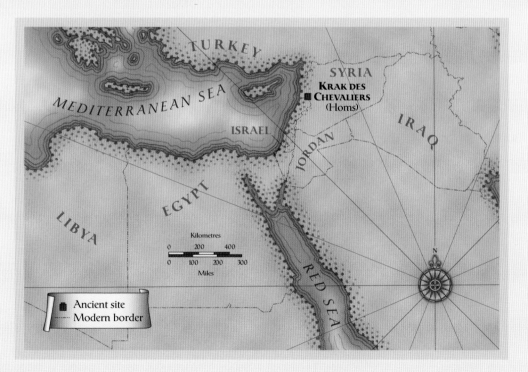

The knights who arrived in the Middle East found themselves deep in enemy territory. They were more than 3,000 km (2,000 miles) from home and were greatly outnumbered by Muslim soldiers.

The crusaders built massive castles where they would be safe. A series of these castles stretched from the mountains of modern Turkey to the hills near Jerusalem.

By far the most famous castle of the crusaders was the Krak des Chevaliers. The name means 'Castle of the Knights'. (*Krak* means 'fortress' in an ancient Middle Eastern language. *Des chevaliers* is French for 'of the knights'.) The castle is in north-western Syria. It has high walls and tall towers. It looks like a castle from a fairy tale such as 'Sleeping Beauty' or 'Cinderella'.

Krak des Chevaliers is surrounded on three sides by steep cliffs.

'The perfect storybook castle that you have always known existed somewhere.'

EVER *Wonder?*

How did soldiers build the crusader castles? After all, the soldiers were trained in fighting, not in building. Actually, soldiers did not build the castles. Skilled stonemasons and other craftsmen travelled from Europe with the crusaders. They enlarged the Krak and built other castles. Some of them were the same craftspeople who built beautiful cathedrals in Europe.

This stone carving from Turkey shows the coat of arms of a group of crusaders known as the Order of Saint John of Jerusalem. The four figures are saints.

A CRAVING FOR CASTLES

The major Crusades took place between 1100 and 1300. The crusaders began to build castles and other fortifications almost as soon as they arrived in the Middle East. The crusaders came from England, France, and other western European countries. They were very familiar with castles. They knew that castles were good fortresses. A few hundred knights in a castle could hold off an army of thousands of enemy soldiers.

In about 1150, a group of crusaders arrived in Syria. This group called themselves the Order of Saint John of Jerusalem, or the Knights Hospitaller. They found an ancient fortress near the modern city of Homs, Syria. The fortress was more than one thousand years old. The knights took over the fortress. They enlarged the building and turned it into a European-style castle – the Krak des Chevaliers.

DO NOT ENTER

The Krak de Chevaliers was surrounded by an outer wall 30 m thick. Three sides of the wall were on the edge of a steep cliff. Inside the outer wall was a second wall. Between the two walls was a moat, or trench, filled with water. A drawbridge crossed the moat. The knights could lower and raise the bridge to let friends enter and keep their enemies out. The inner wall had guard towers where soldiers stood watch.

Behind the inner wall were stone buildings. The buildings had enough living space for about two thousand people. There were also stables big enough to house hundreds of horses. Other buildings included a church, a meeting hall and a giant storage building. In the cliffs behind the castle, the knights dug extra storage chambers for food. A pipe brought fresh water from the mountains into caves underneath the castle. These caves served as water storage tanks.

Left: *The Krak is surrounded by a moat for protection.*
Below: *This view from the top of the castle shows the two walls and the road leading to the castle.*

SEIZING BY SIEGE

The storage buildings and water supply were very important in the Middle Ages. In those days, invaders often surrounded an enemy city or castle in an action called a siege. The siege was a military blockade. By surrounding the castle or city, the invaders prevented food, water and other supplies from reaching the people inside. If the attackers kept the siege going long enough, people inside would have to surrender or starve.

However, the knights at the Krak had large supplies of food and water. Some historians think they had enough supplies to last five years. So they were able to wait out sieges. They did not worry about starvation.

During sieges, enemy soldiers sometimes used battering rams and other heavy equipment. They tried to break through the castle's walls. Soldiers stationed in the Krak's guard towers and along the top of its walls could defend the castle from this kind of attack. From high above ground, the defenders shot arrows at the enemy below or hurled heavy rocks. Sometimes they poured boiling hot water or oil to burn the attackers.

CHAIN OF FORTRESSES

The Krak was a military masterpiece for another reason. It was part of a network of seven castles on the main route between the Mediterranean Sea and Jerusalem. Anyone wishing to move an army or supplies along that route had to go through mountain passes. The seven castles were along those passes.

STINKY *Sieges*

Soldiers attacking a castle during a siege sometimes played dirty tricks on the enemy – dirty, smelly tricks. The attackers saved the bodies of dead horses and camels instead of burying them. They waited until the bodies were rotten and crawling with maggots. Then the attackers used machines called catapults to hurl the dead animals over castle walls. The bodies created a terrible stink inside the castle. Germs from the bodies sometimes made people in the castles fall ill and die.

Soldiers in the castles could easily spot enemies coming through the mountains. When lookouts in one castle spotted an enemy army, they lit big fires on top of the castle walls. Lookouts in the next castle could see the signal fires from far away at night. They lit their own fires to pass on the signal to the next castle, which passed it further along. The soldiers also used fires to call other castles for help when their castle was under attack.

DEFEATED AT LAST

Muslim armies laid siege to the Krak des Chevaliers at least twelve times over a span of 150 years. However, the Krak's defences were too strong and it withstood siege after siege. Muslim armies could never break it.

In 1271 an Egyptian king named Baybars I led his army against the Krak. At the time, only three hundred knights were stationed inside the castle. One story says that King Baybars besieged the Krak for a month with no sign that its soldiers would surrender.

The king was frustrated. He tried a new tactic. He wrote a letter ordering the knights to surrender. He signed the letter with the name of their commander. The knights thought the letter was real. They surrendered without a fight.

KIDS' Crusades?

Stories say that in 1212, a young boy in France and another in Germany recruited thousands of children into an army. The boys convinced other children to make a journey to the Holy Land. Most of the children were under twelve years of age.

They set out on foot, with no horses or weapons *(the illustration below is a French woodcut from 1877 based on a Gustave Doré engraving).* They hoped to take over the Holy Land not with weapons but with their prayers. However, the children never reached their destination. Some stories say that traders sold the children into slavery along the way. Other stories say the children died in a shipwreck in the Mediterranean Sea. There are many different versions of the Children's Crusade story. Nobody knows if it is fact or fiction.

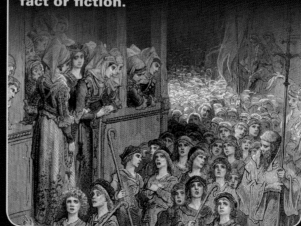

'Perhaps the most . . . admirable castle in the world'
— TE Lawrence, a British soldier and writer, describing the Krak des Chevaliers, 1909

The Krak is one of the most well preserved crusader castles in the world. This passageway still has many of its original details.

After the knights left, King Baybars and other Muslim rulers rebuilt damaged parts of the castle. They added new guard towers. Muslim armies used the Krak as their own fortress until modern times.

A MODERN WONDER

Visitors to modern Syria can still marvel at this ancient wonder. The government of Syria protects and maintains the Krak as a tourist attraction. The Krak is also a UNESCO World Heritage Site. Visitors can tour the castle and its grounds. They can see that the Krak is remarkably well preserved. It looks almost as it did hundreds of years ago, when knights in armour defended it from sieges.

Timeline

c 4000 BC   The Sumerian civilization develops in Mesopotamia.

2000s BC   King Shulgi completes construction of the Great Ziggurat at Ur (in Iraq).

c 965 BC   Solomon becomes the ruler of the kingdom of Israel. He builds a temple in Jerusalem.

668 BC   King Ashurbanipal creates a library in Nineveh (in Iraq).

586 BC   The Babylonians conquer Jerusalem and destroy Solomon's Temple.

559 BC   Cyrus begins conquering surrounding territory and building the Persian Empire.

c 518 BC   King Darius builds Persepolis (in Iran), one of two capitals of the Persian Empire.

400s BC   The Nabataeans begin to build Petra, a city carved out of stone in what is modern-day Jordan.

330 BC   Persepolis falls to the army of Alexander the Great.

20 BC   King Herod remodels the Second Temple in Jerusalem.

c AD 25   The Nabataeans build the Khazneh, or Treasury, in Petra.

70   Roman soldiers destroy the Second Temple in Jerusalem.

532   Justinian orders the building of Hagia Sophia in Constantinople (modern Istanbul, Turkey).

558   The dome of Hagia Sophia collapses.

600s   The Islamic religion develops in the Middle East.

691   Muslims complete construction of the Dome of the Rock in Jerusalem.

c 1100 to 1300   Soldiers march from Europe to the Middle East in the Crusades to capture the Holy Land from Muslim rule.

c 1150   Knights from Europe occupy the Krak des Chevaliers in Syria.

1271 Egyptian king Baybars tricks crusaders at the Krak des Chevaliers into surrendering.

1453 The Ottomans conquer Constantinople. They turn Hagia Sophia into a mosque.

1812 Johann Burckhardt rediscovers the ruins of Petra.

1840s British archaeologists excavate the ruins of Nineveh.

1930s Archaeologists begin excavating the ruins of Persepolis.

1935 The government of Turkey turns Hagia Sophia into a museum.

1967 Israel creates the Western Wall Plaza to give worshippers better access to the Western Wall.

1971 Iranian leaders hold a grand ceremony at Persepolis to celebrate the anniversary of Iran's ancient monarchy.

1979 Persepolis becomes a UNESCO World Heritage Site.

1981 The Old City of Jerusalem, including the Western Wall, becomes a UNESCO World Heritage Site.

1985 Petra becomes a UNESCO World Heritage Site. The historic buildings of Istanbul, including Hagia Sophia, become a World Heritage Site.

2003 The United States invades Iraq. Warfare prevents people from touring the ruins at Ur and Nineveh.

2006 The Krak des Chevaliers becomes a UNESCO World Heritage Site.

2007 A Swiss group holds a contest to name the New Seven Wonders of the World. The new list includes Petra.

CHOOSE AN EIGHTH WONDER

Now that you've read about the seven wonders of the ancient Middle East, do a little research to choose an eighth wonder. Or make a list with your friends, and vote to see which wonder is your favourite.

To do your research, look at some of the websites and books listed in the Further Reading and Websites section of this book. Look for places in the ancient Middle East that
- *have an interesting history*
- *were difficult to make at the time or required new technology*
- *were extra big or tall*
- *were hidden from view or unknown to foreigners for many centuries*

You might even try gathering photos and writing your own chapter on the eighth wonder!

GLOSSARY AND PRONUNCIATION GUIDE

archaeologists: scientists who study buildings, tools and other remains of ancient cultures

artefacts: statues, tools, weapons and other objects remaining from ancient cultures

Bible: a collection of ancient writings that is sacred to both Jews and Christians

caravan: a group of travellers who, in ancient times, relied on camels and other animals to carry heavy loads

cathedral: a large Christian church that serves as headquarters for all the churches in a district

city-state: an independent state consisting of a city and the surrounding territory

civilization: an advanced society with systems of government, defence, communications, culture and technology

Crusades: a series of expeditions in the Middle Ages in which soldiers from Europe tried to recapture the Holy Land in the Middle East from Muslim rule

cuneiform: a writing system used in the ancient Middle East. Texts were written by carving wedge-shaped letters into wet clay tablets.

excavate: to dig up artefacts or structures that have been buried by dirt, rock and sand

monument: a building, statue or other large structure

mosaic: a picture made from small pieces of coloured glass, stone, or other material

mosque: an Islamic house of worship

Muslims: people who practise the Islamic religion

provinces: small territories into which a kingdom or nation is divided

reservoir: a pond or lake used to store large amounts of water

ruins: the remains of a destroyed city or group of buildings

scribes: ancient workers who were specially trained to read and write

siege: a military manoeuvre in which an invading army surrounds a city or fortification. The invaders keep food and supplies from reaching those inside.

terrace: a wide, flat platform on the side of a building

SOURCE NOTES

8   AncientWorlds, 'Mesopotamia', *AncientWorlds*, 2007, http://www.ancientworlds.net/
    aw/Homesite Room/10290 (8 August 2007).

10 Chris Scarre, ed., *The Seventy Wonders of the Ancient World: The Great Monuments and
    How They Were Built* (London: Thames and Hudson, 2000) 20.

14 Agatha Christie, *Agatha Christie: An Autobiography* (New York: Dodd, Mead and
    Company, 1977) 364.

19 Andrew Lawler, 'Bringing a Long-Lost Library Back to Life', *Science*, 2 May 2002, 834.

21 AncientWorlds.

28 Shapour Suren-Pahlav, ed., 'Cyrus Charter of Human Rights', *Iran Chamber Society*, 31
    October 2007, http://www.iranchamber.com/history/cyrus/cyrus_charter.php (22 July
    2007).

29 Iran Chamber Society, 'Parse or Persepolis', *Iran Chamber Society*, 31 October 2007,
    http://www.iranchamber.com/history/persepolis/persepolis1.php (19 August 2007).

31 Charles-Emmanuel Douxuan, 'The Mystery of Persepolis', *UNESCO Courier*, 1 May
    1995, http://www.accessmylibrary.com/coms2/summary_0286-9372096_ITM (28
    November 2007).

38 Israel Antiquities Authority, 'The Babylonian Talmud, *Bava Bathra* 4a', *Jerusalem
    Archaeological Park*, n.d., http://www.archpark.org.il/article.asp?period_id=1&id=31
    (8 August 2007).

46 Johann Ludwig Burckhardt, *Travels in Syria and the Holy Land* (London: John Murray,
    1822), 421–431.

49 Atlas Travel and Tourist Agency, 'Petra Maps and Monuments', *Atlas Tours*, 2007,
    http://www.atlastours.net/jordan/petra_map.html (29 July 2007).

50 Scarre, *Seventy Wonders*, 68.

53 Richard Usborne, 'Carving Their Names on the Walls of Time', *Saudi Aramco World*,
    March–April 1976, http://www.saudiaramcoworld.com/issue/197602/carving.their
    .names.on.the.walls.of.time.htm (27 November 2007).

56 Lord Kinross, *Hagia Sophia* (New York: Newsweek Books, 1972), 15.

57 W. Lethaby and H. Swainson, trans., 'Procopius on the Great Church', *Medieval
    Sourcebook*, 1996, http://www.fordham.edu/halsall/source/procop-deaed1.html
    (31 October 2007).

59 Ibid.

64 William Tracy, 'Stones That Did the Work of Men', *The Levant*, 1997, http://almashriq
    .hiof.no/syria/600/620/623/the_work_of_men/ (12 August 2007).

69 Robin Fedden, 'The Mountain of the Knights', *Saudi Aramco World*, May–June 1970,
    12–15.

SELECTED BIBLIOGRAPHY

Anker, Charlotte, ed. *Mesopotamia: The Mighty Kings.* Alexandria, VA: Time-Life Books, 1995.

Burton, Rosemary, and Richard Cavendish. *Wonders of the World: 100 Great Man-Made Treasures of Civilization.* New York: Metro Books, 2003.

Cantor, Norman F. *Antiquity: The Civilization of the Ancient World.* New York: HarperCollins, 2003.

Fagan, Brian M., ed. *The Oxford Companion to Archaeology.* New York: Oxford University Press, 1996.

Hunt, Norman Bancroft. *Historical Atlas of Ancient Mesopotamia.* New York: Checkmark Books, 2004.

Kinross, Lord. *Hagia Sophia.* New York: Newsweek Books, 1972.

Lawrence, Bonnie, ed. *The Wonders of the World.* Washington, DC: National Geographic Society, 1998.

Nicolle, David. *Historical Atlas of the Islamic World.* New York: Checkmark Books, 2003.

Reader's Digest. *Vanished Civilizations.* New York: Reader's Digest, 2002.

Renfrew, Lord, and Paul G Bahn, eds. *The Cambridge Illustrated History of Archaeology.* Cambridge: Cambridge University Press, 1999.

Roaf, Michael. *Cultural Atlas of Mesopotamia and the Ancient Near East.* New York: Facts On File, 1990.

Scarre, Chris, ed. *The Seventy Wonders of the Ancient World: The Great Monuments and How They Were Built.* London: Thames and Hudson, 2000.

Stefoff, Rebecca. *Finding the Lost Cities.* New York: Oxford University Press. 1997.

Taylor, Jane. *Petra and the Lost Kingdom of the Nabataeans.* Cambridge, MA: Harvard University Press. 2002.

Westwood, Jennifer. *Atlas of Mysterious Places.* London: Marshall Editions, 1987.

FURTHER READING AND WEBSITES

Books and Magazines

Barnes, Trevor and Tony Robinson. *Archaeology* (Kingfisher Knowledge) 2007. This book has loads of information for anyone interested in learning about archaeology, including where and how to do it.

Cavendish, Richard and Rosemary Burton. *100 Great Wonders of the World* Automobile Association, 2004.This picture book contains full-colour photographs of some of the greatest wonders on Earth.

Christie, Agatha. *Murder in Mesopotamia* (Hercule Poirot Mysteries) Agatha Christie spent time on an archaeological excavation in Ur with her archaeologist husband. She uses this setting as background for this mystery novel.

Hibbert, Adam. *100 Things You Should Know About World Wonders* (100 Things You Should Know About) Miles Kelly Publishing Limited, 2005. You can use this book to find out more about wonders all around the world, including the Incas and Machu Picchu and the Nazca people and their drawings.

Hoffman, Mary. *Seven Wonders of the Ancient World* Frances Lincoln Children's Books, 2004. In this book you can learn about the original seven wonders that Herodotus chose, and find out what makes each one so impressive.

Schomp, Virginia. *Ancient Mesopotamia: The Sumerians, Babylonians and Assyrians* (People of the Ancient World), Franklin Watts, 2005.Use this book to find out more about the culture, religion and society of ancient Mesopotamia.

Shuter, Jane. *Mesopotamia* (Excavating the Past) Heinemann Library, 2005.This book gives you the opportunity to explore the ruins of Mesopotamia and find out more about the lives of the people who lived there.

The Usborne Internet-linked Encyclopedia of the Ancient World (Usborne Internet Linked) Usborne Publishing Limited, 2005.This book contains information about the ancient civilizations of the world. It is linked to a website where you can find more resources, take quizzes and do activities.

Wiltshire, Katharine. *The Pocket Timeline of Ancient Mesopotamia* (British Museum Pocket Timeline) British Museum Press, 2005. This fold-out timeline will help you chart the rise and demise of the Mesopotamian civilizations and will give you the opportunity to learn more about the region's cities, arts and crafts, buildings, religion and learning

Websites

Ancient Mesopotamia

http://www.mesopotamia.co.uk

This comprehensive website has information on many different aspects of life in Mesopotamia. It has explore and learn sections, as well as games which are designed to test your knowledge of the Sumer, Babylonian and Assyrian people. You can even have a go at building your own ziggurat.

BBC History – Ancient Cultures- Mesopotamia

http://www.bbc.co.uk/history/ancient/cultures/mesopotamia_gallery.shtml

This website hosts lots of information on the Mespotamian people, including the people of Sumer and Babylonia.

Mesopotamia

http://www.mesopotamia.co.uk/menu.html

The British Museum maintains this site, which will tell you about the ancient civilizations of the Middle East. Visitors can click on pictures to see various aspects of life in Assyria, Babylonia and Sumer.

World Heritage List

http://whc.unesco.org/en/list

The United Nations Educational, Scientific and Cultural Organization (UNESCO) offers a list of World Heritage Sites online. Many of the listings, including those for Petra and Persepolis, include media clips and additional information.

The World Museum, Liverpool

http://www.liverpoolmuseums.org.uk/wml/humanworld/worldcultures/

On this museum's website you can look at artefacts from different ancient civilizations and find out more about how they were made.

INDEX

ABOUT THE AUTHORS

Michael Woods is a science and medical journalist in Washington, DC, USA, who has won many national writing awards. Mary B Woods is a school librarian. Their past books include the *Ancient Technology* and *Disasters!* series. The Woods have four children. When not writing, reading or enjoying their grandchildren, the Woods travel to gather material for future books.

PHOTO ACKNOWLEDGEMENTS

The images in this book are used with the permission of: © Richard Ashworth/Robert Harding Picture Library Ltd./Alamy, p 6; © Laura Westlund/Independent Picture Service, pp 7, 17, 25, 35, 45, 55, 63; © Scala/Art Resource, NY, p 8; © Bildarchiv Preussischer Kulturbesitz/Art Resource, NY, pp 9 (both), 11 (bottom); PennMuseum image #8750, p 11 (top); © Image Asset Management Ltd./SuperStock, p 12; © The British Museum/Art Resource, NY, pp 13 (top left and bottom right), 19, 28; PennMuseum image #151000, p 13 (top right); © Walter Rawlings/Robert Harding Picture Library Ltd./Alamy, p 13 (bottom left); © Nico Tondini/Robert Harding World Imagery/Getty Images, p 14, 72 (bottom right); © University of East Anglia p 15; © Jane Sweeney/Lonely Planet Images/Getty Images, p 16; © Mary Evans Picture Library/Alamy, p 18; © The Print Collector/Alamy, p 20; © Erich Lessing/Art Resource, NY, pp 21, 48, 57, 58 (bottom); © Assyrian/The Bridgeman Art Library/Getty Images, pp 23, 72 (centre right); The Art Archive/Alfredo Dagli Orti, p 24; © Stefan Baum/Dreamstime.com, p 26; © SEF/Art Resource, NY, p 27; © akg-images/Gérard Degeorge, p 29; © O'Brien World Pictures/Photoshot, p 30 (top); Oriental Institute of the University of Chicago, p 30 (bottom); © Olaf M.Teßmer/Bildarchiv Preussischer Kulturbesitz/Art Resource, NY, p 31; © Bettmann/CORBIS, p 32; © World Pictures/Photoshot, p 33; © Image Select/Art Resource, NY, p 34; © Time & Life Pictures/Getty Images, pp 36, 37; © age fotostock/SuperStock, p 39; Eric Matson/The State of Israel National Photo Collection, p 40 (top); AP Photo, p 40 (bottom); © Menahem Kahana/AFP/Getty Images, p 41 (top); © Zev Radovan/www.BibleLandPictures.com, p 41 (bottom); © Eitan Simanor/Alamy, p 42; © Jon Arnold/Taxi/Getty Images, p 43; © Cindy Miller/Alamy, p 44; © Alexandr Tkachuk/Dreamstime.com, p 46; © DeA Picture Library/Getty Images, p 47; © Alena Yakusheva/Dreamstime.com, p 49; © Dario Bajurin/Dreamstime.com, p 51 (top left); © akg-images/Jean-Louis Nou, p 51 (top right); © Richard Ross/The Image Bank/Getty Images, p 51 (bottom); © Shai Eynav/SuperStock, p 52; © Nexus7/Dreamstime.com, pp 54, 58 (top); © Hazlan Abdul Hakim/Dreamstime.com, p 56; © Joan Coll/Dreamstime.com, p 60; © Ed Freeman/The Image Bank/Getty Images, p 61 (top); © Maxfx/Dreamstime.com, p 61 (bottom); © DEA/G DAGLI ORTI/Getty Images, p 62, 64, 72 (top centre); © Ancient Art & Architecture Collection, Ltd., p 65; © Richard Ross/The Image Bank/Getty Images, p 66 (top); © Mirafilm/Dreamstime.com, p 66 (bottom); © akg-images, p 68; © Steve Roxbury/Danita Delimont/Alamy, p 69; © Robert Harding/Digital Vision/Getty Images, p 72 (top left); © Mia Klein/Iconica/Getty Images, p 72 (top right); © ALIKI SAPOUNTZI/aliki image library/Alamy, p 72 (bottom left); © German School/The Bridgeman Art Library/Getty Images, p 72 (bottom centre).

Front Cover: © Robert Harding/Digital Vision/Getty Images (top left); © DEA/G. DAGLI ORTI/Getty Images (top centre); © Mia Klein/Iconica/Getty Images (top right); © German School/The Bridgeman Art Library/Getty Images (centre); © Assyrian/The Bridgeman Art Library/Getty Images (bottom left); © ALIKI SAPOUNTZI/aliki image library/Alamy (bottom centre); © Nico Tondini/Robert Harding World Imagery/Getty Images (bottom right).